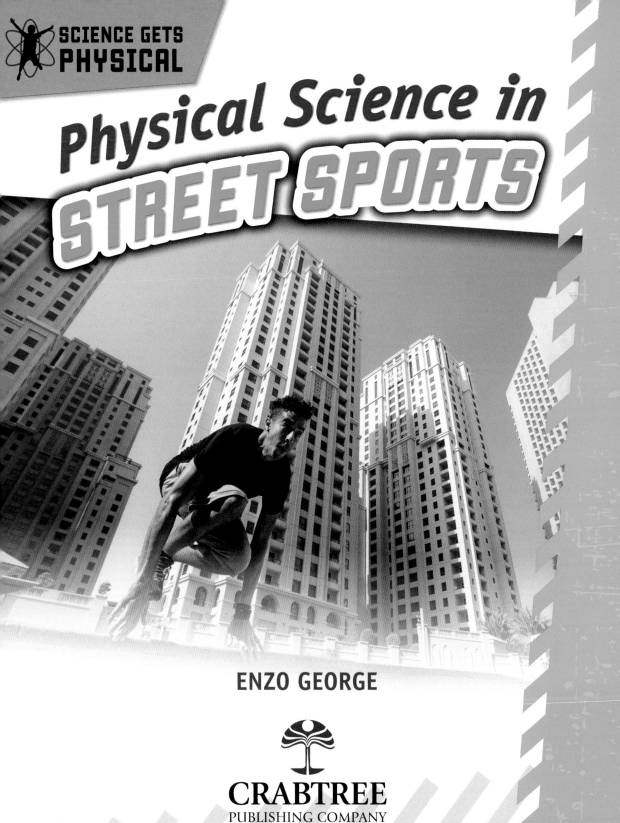

# SCIENCE GETS PHYSICAL

# Physical Science in STREET SPORTS

ENZO GEORGE

## CRABTREE
PUBLISHING COMPANY
WWW.CRABTREEBOOKS.COM

**Author:** Enzo George
**Editors:** Sarah Eason, Jennifer Sanderson,
    and Elizabeth DiEmanuele
**Consultant:** David Hawksett
**Editorial director:** Kathy Middleton
**Proofreader:** Wendy Scavuzzo
**Design:** Paul Myerscough and Jeni Child
**Design edits:** Katherine Berti
**Cover design:** Lorraine Inglis
**Photo research:** Rachel Blount
**Print and production coordinator:**
    Katherine Berti

Written, developed, and produced by Calcium

**Photo Credits:**
**Inside**: Inside: Shutterstock: 5 second Studio: p. 44; Paul
Aiken: p. 31; Alexapicso: p. 45; Aaron Amat: p. 27; AstroStar:
p. 28; Sergei Bachlakov: p. 11; Galina Barskaya: p. 8; Rick
Becker-Leckrone: p. 15; Bluecrayola: p. 19, 20; BluIz60: p. 4;
Coka: p. 34; Fernanda photos: p. 36; Stanislav Fridkin: p. 3,
25; HomeArt: p. 10; hurricanehank : p. 24; Yeongsik Im: p. 29;
lzf: p. 16; A Katz: p. 40, 41; KlaraBstock: p. 37; Jacob Lund: p.
9; Brian McEntire: p. 23; Doug McLean: p. 21; Muzsy: p. 42;
Nejron Photo: p. 39; Nikolay100: p. 38; Oneinchpunch: p. 32;
Rawpixel.com: p. 43; Stefan Schurr: p. 26; Syda Productions:
p. 33; Sylv1rob1: p. 13; Taboga: p. 12; Taras-studio: p. 1, 30;
Vagengeim: p. 35; Vladeep: p. 14; Monika Wisniewska: p. 7;
Yanik88: p. 5; Wikimedia Commons: Bengt Nyman: p. 22;
Karen Roe: p. 18; TobiasK: p. 17
**Cover:** Shutterstock: Dan Holm

**Library and Archives Canada Cataloguing in Publication**

Title: Physical science in street sports / Enzo George.
Names: George, Enzo, author.
Description: Series statement: Science gets physical |
    Includes index.
Identifiers: Canadiana (print) 20190195479 |
    Canadiana (ebook) 20190195487 |
    ISBN 9780778775485 (hardcover) |
    ISBN 9780778776512 (softcover) |
    ISBN 9781427125231 (HTML)
Subjects: LCSH: Sports—Juvenile literature.
Classification: LCC GV705.4 .G46 2020 | DDC j796—dc23

**Library of Congress Cataloging-in-Publication Data**

CIP available at the Library of Congress

LCCN: 2019043962

# Crabtree Publishing Company
www.crabtreebooks.com    1-800-387-7650

Printed in the U.S.A./012020/CG20191115

**Published in Canada**
**Crabtree Publishing**
616 Welland Ave.
St. Catharines, Ontario
L2M 5V6

**Published in the United States**
**Crabtree Publishing**
PMB 59051
350 Fifth Avenue, 59th Floor
New York, New York 10118

**Published in the United Kingdom**
**Crabtree Publishing**
Maritime House
Basin Road North, Hove
BN41 1WR

**Published in Australia**
**Crabtree Publishing**
Unit 3 - 5 Currumbin Court
Capalaba
QLD 4157

# CONTENTS

# CHAPTER 1

# SPORTS ON THE STREET

**P**eople have played sports on streets for many centuries. After all, the laws of **physics** make them a great place for sports. Walls and steps can be used in all kinds of activities. Street sports work not only because of **friction**, but also **forces**, the laws of motion, **inertia**, and **torque**. It turns out that streets are a physics playground!

## A Long History

Some street sports are older than others. One of the most popular used to be soapbox racing. Children built their own cars from wooden soap boxes or fruit crates. They might add four wheels from an old bicycle or stroller. Then they held **derbies**, where they raced their cars down sloping streets. Today, soapbox racing is not as common, but it is still popular. There are many organized events and even some permanent tracks.

Official soapbox derbies have been held in the United States since 1934. Competitors race in handmade vehicles down sloping streets.

In the past, roller derbies were also popular. People raced on four-wheeled roller skates. In the 1960s, inline skates appeared. On inline skates, wheels were a single line on each skate. Inline skates made roller sports even more popular. They could be used just like ice skates, but on the streets, for racing and roller hockey.

## New Sports

Another sport appeared in the 1960s and it grew fast. Surfers in California wanted something to do in bad weather, so they put small surfboards on their roller skates. Skateboarding has come a long way since then.

Today, there are more than 11 million skateboarders in the world. Skateboarders use physics. Friction and **velocity** help them race fast and perform stunts.

Parkour athletes also look for ways to beat **gravity.** Their stunts look amazing, but they can be dangerous—even deadly.

## Street Science

Street sports do not have to be dangerous. When you see a game of hoops, street football, or handball, you are seeing physics in action.

*A skater rides a longboard. This is a type of skateboard that is built for speed and cruising.*

# Street Environment

It is important to remember that the streets can be dangerous. Playing sports on the streets made sense in the past. There were fewer cars on the roads, so streets were empty most of the time. Things are different now. There are cars and bikes driving past and pedestrians on the sidewalks. Always put safety first when playing any games on the street.

## Dedicated Spaces

To be safe, many street sports do not take place near the street itself. They are only called street sports because of where they began. Now there are skate parks, roller tracks, and courts to shoot hoops. Many cities also have large public spaces that people use to play sports. Some people prefer to be in areas built for sports. These are made for safety and do not bother others. But, some sports fans prefer to stay on the street. They like the challenge of adapting to an environment that is not meant for sports. Some also enjoy the thrill of doing something that they are not supposed to do.

Skate parks are a safe environment for learning tricks. They often have slopes, ramps, and rails on which to practice.

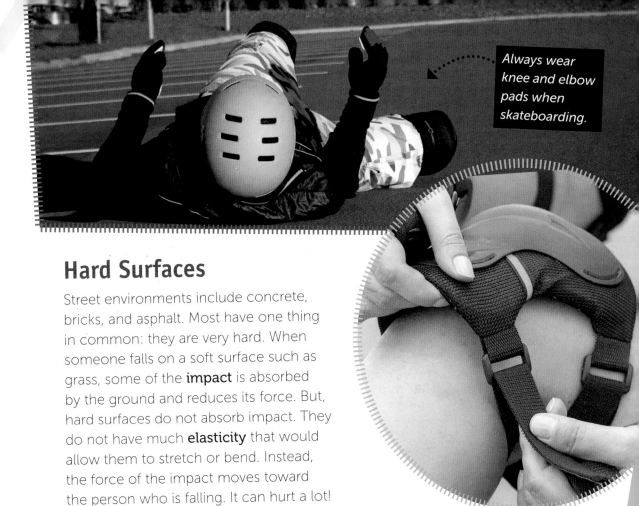

*Always wear knee and elbow pads when skateboarding.*

## Hard Surfaces

Street environments include concrete, bricks, and asphalt. Most have one thing in common: they are very hard. When someone falls on a soft surface such as grass, some of the **impact** is absorbed by the ground and reduces its force. But, hard surfaces do not absorb impact. They do not have much **elasticity** that would allow them to stretch or bend. Instead, the force of the impact moves toward the person who is falling. It can hurt a lot!

## GETTING PHYSICAL: PROTECTIVE GEAR

Falling over is never fun. On a hard surface, it can be painful and also very serious. A hit on the side of the head from a curb or a step can even be deadly. Urban athletes whose sports rely on speed and balance, such as skateboarders and inline skaters, wear protective gear. They wear helmets with a hard shell surrounding foam padding that molds itself to the head. In case of impact, the shell shatters, which has the effect of transferring shock away from the skull. The foam deforms to absorb more of the shock. Many street athletes wear cuplike pads over their knees and elbows. These joints are not protected by a lot of flesh. So, a hit to them can be very painful.

# CHAPTER 2

# SKATEBOARDING

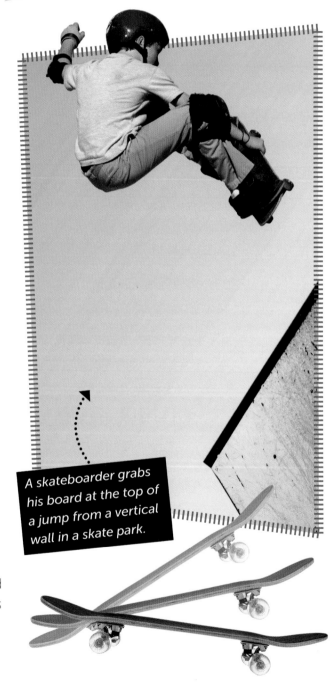

A skateboarder grabs his board at the top of a jump from a vertical wall in a skate park.

One of the most popular street sports in the world is skateboarding. You can often find a small square or urban space with a group of riders. They may be trying out new tricks, jumping down steps, or sliding their boards along metal poles. Today, there are many skate parks which have tubes and ramps designed for the sport. In the past, many skaters started by finding places to practice in quiet parts of the city or town.

## More than a Board on Wheels

A skateboard seems simple. But, there is a lot more to it. A skateboard has design features that use physics. Riders also use **kinetic energy**, friction, **aerodynamics**, and **levers** to move. They even use these parts of physics to beat gravity. Gravity is the force that pulls everything to the ground.

# Helping the Rider

Every part of the skateboard is designed to help the rider. The board itself, called the deck, is not flat. It rises slightly at each end. The shape allows the rider to press down on the slope to lift the opposite end of the board into the air. There is usually tape on the deck that has a rough surface. The roughness creates a larger surface area, so there is more friction between the deck and the skater's shoes to create more grip. Beneath the deck, the wheels are attached to two trucks. Each truck holds a fixed **axle**. But, it is hinged where it is joined to the deck. That means it is variably **flexible**. Pressing down on the deck makes the axle swivel. If the rider leans to the left, the left side of the deck presses closer to the floor. The effect on the joint of the truck is to make the axle **pivot** toward the left, steering the board. The tiny wheels are made of urethane. As the board rolls along, they flatten a little, then return to being fully circular. This helps reduce the **drag** from the ground, known as **rolling resistance**.

A skateboarder uses their hand to steady themselves as they get ready to take a bend on a country road. The skateboarder wears gloves to protect their hands.

# The Deck

There is more to the deck than just bright logos. Most decks are concave. This means that they rise at the front and back, and also toward each edge. This shape gives the rider control. The rider can easily cause it to steer or tip in a direction. All they have to do is press their foot against the inclined part of the deck.

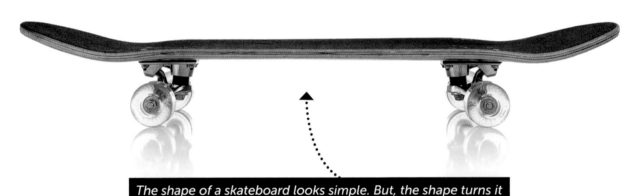

The shape of a skateboard looks simple. But, the shape turns it into a series of levers by making the two axles work as pivots.

## Molded Shape

Many boards are made from maple wood. Maple wood is strong. It is also flexible enough to bend rather than break while the rider is doing tricks. The wood's natural flexibility increases from adding five to seven thin layers of wood. Together, these layers form the deck. Each layer can adjust slightly, while the other layers hold the board together. The boards are stuck together under high pressure. The pressure molds the wood into its concave shape.

## Variations

The rises at each end of the deck are known as kicktails. But, the one at the front of the board is usually called the nose and the one at the back is called the tail. The overall outline of the skateboard is called its plan. The wider the deck, the more stable the board usually is. Most standard skateboards are 7 to 10.5 inches (18 to 27 cm) wide and 28 to 33 inches (71 to 84 cm) long.

*Racers in a longboard race in Canada wear leather suits to protect them if they slide across the ground.*

Some riders prefer a much longer skateboard, known as a longboard. A longboard is good for riding fast, but not as useful for doing tricks. A longboard also travels over rough ground more smoothly than a shorter board. Its longer space between the front and back wheels allows it to absorb bumps and remain more stable. Smaller plastic boards, known as Penny boards, are named after the Australian company that designed them. They are lighter than normal skateboards, but just as strong.

## GETTING PHYSICAL: GRIP TAPE

Skaters cover the top of their deck with a layer of rough tape to give them more grip. The grip tape has a surface that is a little like sandpaper. The gritty effect comes from different particles, such as silicon carbide or aluminum oxide, which are stuck with resin on a sheet of plastic. This is called PVC. The particles are different sizes, and can be as small as table salt or as big as peppercorns. They also have different sharpnesses. The grains increase the surface area of the board, and add friction to the sole of the rider's shoe. This makes it easier to steer the board and perform stunts.

# The Truck

The main parts of the skateboard are the two trucks that hold the wheels beneath the deck. They seem like simple axles, but they are flexible. They act differently from a fixed axle.

## Essential Component

The truck consists of a baseplate that is connected to the underside of the deck with screws. The baseplate holds a kingpin, which in turn holds a crosspiece known as the hanger. The hanger contains the axle. It is pivoted, so it can tip to one side or the other. This pivot forces the axle to rotate, creating a force called torque, which makes the board turn. The rider steers by leaning to one side or the other, causing the board to dip. This makes the front axle pivot to that side. At the same time, the rear axle mounts in the opposite direction, so it pivots in the opposite direction. If the front axle pivots to the right, the rear axle pivots to the left. This brings the wheels on the right side of the board closer together. It also brings the wheels on the left side farther apart and turns the skateboard in an arc.

The screw in the middle of the truck can be adjusted, depending on the type of skating the boarder wants to do.

Skateboard wheels come in different sizes and hardnesses. Larger wheels help smooth out cracks in uneven ground. Smaller wheels are easier to **accelerate** and keep the board's **center of mass** low, making the board more stable. Harder wheels respond more quickly, and are useful for doing tricks. Softer wheels have more grip. They are great for an easy ride. Almost all skateboard wheels are made of a hard material called **polyurethane**. They have seven ball **bearings** inside to help them turn easily on their axle, which reduces friction.

Small wheels are only about 2 inches (5 cm). Small wheels are better for tricks than they are for long rides.

## Making a Ride Comfortable

The trucks are flexible. The hanger is held in place with bushings, which are rubbery rings that fit on the kingpin, one above and one below the hanger. Riders can tighten or loosen the bushings based on the type of ride. If the bushings are tighter, the rubber is compressed and becomes stiffer. This makes the trucks difficult to turn, but can help with tricks. If the bushings are looser, it is easier to ride and turn. Riders may choose looser bushings for a smoother ride, but at high speeds, that is not always a good thing. A board with loose trucks traveling fast will start to wobble from side to side. If the rider does not slow down, this wobble will grow stronger until it becomes uncontrollable. By that time, the ride is likely to end in disaster.

# Moving and Steering

A skateboard is a machine. It transfers kinetic energy from the rider to the rolling velocity of the wheels. This was all explained more than 350 years ago by a scientist who had never seen a skateboard. His name was Isaac Newton.

## Newton's Laws of Motion

Newton explained all motion with three laws. Newton's First Law says that an object will remain at rest or moving at the same speed in a straight line until it is affected by an external force such as gravity. In physics, this is the definition of inertia. The Second Law explains how the velocity of an object changes when an object is subjected to an external force. The force is the rate at which **momentum** (**mass** x velocity) changes over time. The Third Law says that for every action (or force) in nature, there is an equal and opposite reaction.

## Keep on Rolling!

Newton's laws are at work in skateboarding. When a skateboarder's foot pushes against the ground, the ground pushes back with an equal force. This is Newton's Third Law. The external force of the pushing foot has changed its velocity. This is Newton's Second Law. Now the skateboard is rolling, it will keep rolling unless another force leads it to change. This is Newton's First Law. In the case of a skateboard, we know that gravity and friction will slow down the wheels, as will forces such as **air resistance** and rolling resistance.

Newton's Third Law is at work in skateboarding. When a skateboarder's foot pushes against the ground, the ground pushes back with an equal force.

Many skateboarders use video cameras such as GoPros to record tricks.

## GETTING PHYSICAL: PUMPING

## Riding Along

Once the skateboard is rolling, the rider can keep it going by continuing to push the ground with their foot, or riding down a slope. If the slope is steep enough, the pull of gravity on the board and rider will overcome many forces. This includes friction and the other forces that slow it down. The board will keep rolling to the bottom of the hill.

A skateboard turns when the rider leans. The distribution of their weight transfers through the trucks to the axles, which causes the wheels to turn in one direction or the other. After the turn, the rider's weight returns to being **perpendicular** to the deck and the trucks straighten up.

In a halfpipe or a bowl, skaters need speed to shoot up over the lip to do tricks. But, it is hard to push off the curved ground with their feet.

The answer is pumping. As the board crosses the flattish part of the U-shaped tube, the rider crouches down. Then, they straighten up as the board reaches the bottom of the sloping wall. That increases the rider's energy, which makes the board travel faster. As the board begins to curve upward, **centripetal force** pulls the rider down toward the board. This requires more energy for the rider to straighten up. The work of straightening up gains a little energy for the board and rider so they travel faster. The effect is similar to swinging your legs at the bottom of a swing's arc to "kick" the swing higher.

# Getting Air

Skateboarders seem to be able to defy gravity, but skateboards must obey the forces of physics.

## The Ollie

The ollie is one of the most popular skateboard tricks. In the ollie, the skateboarder jumps into the air, and the skateboard seems to jump with them, as though it is stuck to the skateboarder's feet. The ollie is something every skateboarder learns early on. It looks spectacular, but it is based on an illusion. The skateboarder does nothing to lift the board off the ground.

## Getting It Right

The secret to the stunt is the rise at each end of the board. By pressing down hard on the back end of the board, outside the wheels, the rider jumps to generate torque around the back axle. This force causes the front end of the board to rotate up off the ground. The front is given momentum by the normal forces from the ground, which are equal to the downward force from the skateboarder's foot.

*The ollie was named after its originator, Alan "Ollie" Gelfand. The key to pulling off the perfect ollie is to get your weight on the very tail of the board.*

## Gravity Takes Over

If the board continued to rotate, it would flip up and spin. Instead, the skateboarder uses their other foot to drag against the board to "pull" it up. Then, they push down on the front of the board in the air to stop the rotation. The board's inertia is its tendency to keep moving once its center of mass has momentum. Inertia is what causes it to rise off the ground. The skateboard loses the **angular momentum** that has lifted it into the air. Its velocity drops to zero for a moment and it levels out. At that point, the board is parallel with the ground in midair, with both the rider's feet touching it.

Then, gravity takes over. The skateboard and rider both fall back to the ground, where the boarder's knees bend to absorb the impact. With perfect balance, it is on to the next trick!

*As the tail goes down to the floor, slide your front foot to let the board rotate up off the ground. As you lift your back leg, push down on the nose of the board with your front foot to flatten the board. Get ready for landing!*

## SCIENCE WINS!

### ALDRIN GARCIA'S HIGHEST OLLIE

In February 2011, leading skateboarders from the United States gathered in Las Vegas. They wanted to set a new world record for an ollie. US skateboarder Aldrin Garcia won the $10,000 prize with a new record of 44.5 inches (113 cm). The height was judged using a barrier that skateboarders had to jump over. The record stood until February 2018. Two skaters, Jake Hayes and Xavier Alford, beat the record. They achieved remarkable jumps of 45.5 inches (115.6 cm).

# CHAPTER 3

# SOAPBOX RACING

**Y**ou are at the top of the biggest hill in your neighborhood. Your helmet is on. Ahead of you is a course marked out by bales of straw. Your friends have already started in their own soapbox cars. You have built this special car ready to take on the world. The flag drops, and you're off!

*The drink manufacturer Red Bull sponsors a series of international soapbox car races. These bring in interesting entries, including some that can travel very quickly.*

## A Simple Racer

The simplest soapbox cars are made out of wooden soap crates or fruit crates attached to roller skates. Soapbox cars also have a crossbar for steering in front. The bar has a central pivot, and the rider steers by pulling on ropes. But, some cars have steering wheels, which are useful for steering along a winding course. These are often marked out by straw bales. Cars cannot turn too quickly, or the weight of the rider can

easily cause them to topple over. There is usually a brake, which is often just a lever that pushes a pad against one of the wheels. The friction slows the wheel and the rest of the car slows down, too. At high speeds, this is not always very effective. Crashes are common. In the past, builders took wheels from wherever they could find them, such as from old strollers. Today, it is possible to buy purpose-designed wheels.

## Modern Shapes

The first soapbox cars were open, but the cars have changed. They now have frames of steel covered in a shell made from light plywood, plastic, or other materials. There is one seat for a driver, but some designs have a second seat at the back for a passenger. Soapbox cars have no engines. They are pulled downhill by the force of gravity. Even so, they have been recorded reaching speeds of 101 miles per hour (163 kph). Speeds of 20 to 30 miles per hour (32 to 48 kph) are more common. At such speeds, any kind of crash can be dangerous. Today, riders have to wear crash helmets.

This soapbox car track in Germany is lined with bales of straw to keep the riders from running off the road. It also protects people who are watching.

**S**oapbox cars are sometimes known as gravity racers. That gives a clue about how they work. They are powered only by the pull of gravity, but a first push is sometimes allowed. Once the car is moving, gravity is the force that matters most.

*This car is fitted with a brake beneath that slows it down by increasing friction with the road.*

## Energy Conversion

At the top of its run, the car has **potential energy.** This is the possible energy the car can get from gravity. The amount of potential energy the car has depends on two things. The first is the total weight of the car and rider. The second is the amount of drop from the start of the course to the bottom. Once the car moves, potential energy becomes kinetic, or moving, energy. In most races, they design the track so cars reach their greatest kinetic energy before the end of the race. The best car design is one that quickly converts potential energy to kinetic energy. This means the car can speed up as fast as possible. To do this, car designers have to cut the forces that slow this acceleration by reducing aerodynamic drag and rolling resistance. Aerodynamic drag is the resistance of the **molecules** in the air. Rolling resistance is created by the friction between the wheels and the ground. Vibration of the wheels can also slow it down.

# Watch Your Weight!

When building a soapbox car, there are two things to consider: the weight distribution and the length of the car. The center of mass is the average point where the weight of the car and rider are most intense. This is best in the middle of the car. Having the center of mass evens the weight on both the front and back wheels. This arrangement also reduces the car's **moment of inertia**. Inertia is its resistance to being turned around its central **axis**. The lower the moment of inertia, the faster the car will turn. A low moment of inertia is determined by keeping all weight as close to the center of mass as possible. The farther the weight is from the center of mass, the slower the car.

Thin wheels have low rolling resistance with the ground so they are very quick. However, they are not as stable as thicker wheels.

## GETTING PHYSICAL: FRONT-WHEEL DRIVE

Soapbox cars traditionally have an axle at the front. This axle is steered from the cockpit using a rope that pulls the axle one way or another. In the past, racers often had a long spar (strong pole) in front of the cockpit where the driver's legs rested. The pole created a long distance between the front and rear sets of wheels, but the distance made the cars less stable. The whole car acted like a long lever. The turn of the axle at the front magnified into a larger motion at the rear of the vehicle. The longer the wheelbase, the more the back of the car swung around. A longer wheelbase also made it more difficult to keep the vehicle on the road!

# Crashes

There are many ways to crash a soapbox car! Homemade cars tend to be much better at traveling quickly downhill. While this may add a thrill, it means that crashes are common, so most courses are lined with bales of hay.

For some competitors, wacky vehicles and possible wipeouts are one of the attractions of soapbox car racing!

## Top Speed

The top speed a soapbox car can reach is its **terminal velocity**. Generally, a heavier car will have a higher terminal velocity than a lighter car. This is because gravity places more attraction on a higher mass. Often, the sport will divide cars into classes based on weight. These classes help make the race fair.

To race well, it is important to reduce aerodynamic drag and rolling resistance. The best way to reduce drag is to create a **streamlined** shell that travels smoothly through the air. To do this, the rider's head must stay low so that it does not cause any extra resistance. All surfaces need to be smooth. The widest cross-section of the car (as seen from the front) should be as small as possible. The wheels should align. At their best, the wheels roll perpendicular to the ground without wobbling.

Narrow tires inflated to a higher pressure can reduce rolling resistance. A high air pressure helps the tires keep their shape as they pass over the ground. The larger the tire, the less the rolling resistance. However, changes to the wheels can lessen the grip of the tires, which makes it harder for the driver to steer the best course.

## Fewer Wheels

The simplest way to reduce rolling resistance on a car is by taking off a wheel and building a three-wheeler! That would reduce rolling resistance by one-quarter. If a car could travel with only two wheels, it would have only half the rolling resistance. That is why race rules specify that a soap box car must have four wheels.

## GETTING PHYSICAL: ACCELERATION AND MOMENTUM

A heavier soapbox car and driver will speed up more slowly, but it will reach a higher speed than a lighter car. It has less acceleration, but more momentum. In physics, acceleration is any change in velocity, such as speeding up, slowing down, or changing direction while in motion. The rate at which a soapbox car speeds up from a standing start depends mostly on its mass. The mass of the car is pulled by gravity. Once a car is rolling, momentum, or how much motion it has, is produced by multiplying its mass by its velocity. This gives a higher momentum for a heavier vehicle.

*Wearing a streamlined helmet helps reduce air resistance and is vital for safety.*

# CHAPTER 4

# INLINE SKATING

**W**e already know that Isaac Newton came up with Laws of Motion. These laws showed how a skateboard works before the skateboard was even invented. His laws also show how another invention works: skates. Wheeled skates were invented 60 years after Newton's time.

## Two Types of Skates

The first roller skates had three wheels and were based on ice skates. Later roller skates had two pairs of wheels at the front and back. To slide, they had to reduce the friction between the wheels and the ground. Small wheels designed to roll as smoothly as possible reduced any drag on the ground. Modern inline skates normally have four wheels arranged in a line down the center of the skate. They look a little like the blade of an ice skate. Inline skates are easier to balance on than the first skates and roll more quickly.

*Inline skaters perform a wide variety of jumps and tricks. But, they should always wear a helmet!*

# Moving Forward

Newton's Laws of Motion apply to the creation of forward energy in skating. When you push backward with your skate, you move forward. This is Newton's Third Law: for every action there is an equal and opposite reaction. To make the push better, your foot needs to be at a slight angle. If your feet are pointing directly forward, all that will happen is that you will roll backward.

There are many types of street skating. Some are just for fun, such as roller skating with friends. Others are more organized. There is artistic skating and roller hockey, which is like hockey on wheels. There is downhill skating. Slalom skating is when competitors weave through a series of gates that set a winding course. There are also stunts and jumps like the moves seen in ice skating.

Speedskating is a serious sport, with international competitions.

# Motion and Balance

When skating, it is far easier to stay upright when you are moving than when you are still. The spinning of the wheels makes it easier to balance.

## Keep Spinning

A spinning wheel creates a **gyroscopic** effect. A gyroscope is a wheel that spins on an axle that can swing in any direction. When the gyroscope spins, it always tries to return to its starting position. On skates, this means if the spinning wheels tip to one side or the other, they try to return to an upright position. The result? Better balance for the skater.

As one leg pushes out, the skater's arms move in the other direction. Their mass also shifts toward the leading leg.

# GETTING PHYSICAL: ROLLER SKATES VERSUS INLINE SKATES

As you can see from the picture on the right, the four wheels on a roller skate are placed in a square shape. This creates a center of balance in the approximate middle of the boot. On an inline skate, the center of balance is also in the middle of the boot, but there are no wheels left and right of it to provide support and spread the skater's weight. That leaves the skater's weight concentrated on a narrower base. That means the skate is less stable.

## Keep Your Balance

The skater helps their own balance by moving their body or throwing out their arms. This may all happen by instinct, but the movements are controlled by math. Skaters might not know it, but they are trying to increase their moment of inertia to help them stay up. This is similar to the way tightrope walkers carry very long horizontal poles to balance.

An object's moment of inertia measures how easy or hard it is to make that object rotate around an axis. The lower the moment of inertia, the easier it is for the object to rotate around a pivot. When you are on skates, your pivot point is your feet. When you overbalance, they stay in place while your body rotates around them. By putting out your arms to the sides, you are moving more of your mass away from the pivot point of your feet, which raises the moment of inertia. That makes it harder for you to rotate, but a higher moment of inertia also means it is harder to stop!

# Friction and Braking

There is a rubber stopper at the back of the wheels that acts as a brake when the skater lifts the front of their foot.

**I**f you stand on the ground in your shoes, raise one leg, then the other, then spin around, you will probably be okay. But, if you try doing this wearing skates, you will probably fall. The reason for this is friction.

## Sticking Point

When you are wearing shoes, there is a lot of friction between your feet and the ground. This helps you "stick" to the ground. It also helps you keep your balance. With skates, the wheels have very little friction, so there is no force to hold your feet still. Unless you are a good skater or you have amazing balance, they will shoot out from under you.

## Easy Roller

Skate wheels are usually made from polyurethane. This material is a type of hard plastic that does not wear quickly and has low rolling resistance. The wheels are hollow and they contain small ball bearings packed with grease.

The grease supports the wheels as they turn around the axle and lessen friction. If you hold a ball tight while you push it over the ground, it will create friction. But, if you let it go so it can roll, it travels easily. The ball bearings in skate wheels do the same thing. They let the wheel travel with as little resistance as possible. Bearings are usually made from polished steel or ceramic and are made to roll as smoothly as possible. This means that a skater can travel easily over the ground. The bearings also help support and distribute the skater's weight on the wheels. They also resist wear from the rapid revolution of the wheels.

# Using Friction

When it is time to stop, skaters need to create friction. On inline skates, they do this by applying a hard rubber brake to the ground by lifting the front of their foot. The block is in back of the skate. Some roller skates also have a rubber brake at the front to assist in tricks and dance moves. Some skaters stop by turning one of their feet perpendicular to their direction of travel. This again creates friction. The forward energy of the skater changes to heat energy and releases it into the air.

## SCIENCE WINS!

### ITALY'S TEAM TACTICS

Italy's inline skaters hold many world records on the track and on the road. In team events, the Italians, like other teams, work together to win. The team members form a paceline. This is when they all skate close together in a line. In a paceline, the lead skater experiences the most drag. The skaters stay behind the leader, who shelters them from the air resistance. This allows the team to save energy. Skaters take turns at the front of the line, protecting their fastest team member. When they near the finish, their fastest member is ready to make a dash for the line.

Teams train together so they get used to skating close together to reduce the drag on skaters farther back in the group.

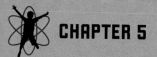

# CHAPTER 5

# PARKOUR

**H**ave you seen videos of young people running and jumping their way across the city? Were they leaping over railings or somersaulting over benches? Jumping from roof to roof? Welcome to the street sport of parkour! Parkour can be very dangerous. It should only be performed by someone who is well trained in the sport. Let's take a look at the physical science behind the stunts.

## Assault Course

The sport developed in France in the 1980s. It started as a challenge to cross an urban environment as fast as possible. The goal was to do so without using any equipment.

In some ways, it resembles the obstacle courses used to train the military. In those courses, soldiers have to climb walls and crawl through pipes.

*Parkour athletes turn unlikely obstacles into sports equipment.*

Parkour athletes are skilled at using the mechanics of their bodies to clear obstacles. They make leaping over large objects seem incredibly easy!

## Overcoming Force

Parkour athletes share skills found in other sports. This is especially true with athletics and gymnastics. Parkour athletes need to gain speed and maintain it as they change direction. They need excellent balance. They also need to be aware of the forces acting on their bodies. Force helps parkour athletes maintain their forward momentum. The most important of those forces is gravity. Parkour has a lot of vaulting and jumping.

In vaulting, the athletes use their arms or legs to spring into the air to clear obstacles. Some moves take place high off the ground! Athletes jump from the top of one narrow wall to the top of another, over a high drop. This requires great skill and balance. It also requires a lot of practice in safe surroundings. Never try stunts like this yourself.

# Clearing Obstacles

**B**enches, railings, steps, planters, outdoor staircases. For a parkour athlete, every part of an urban landscape is a potential obstacle that can slow him or her down. So, they learn many skills to get past them. Sometimes, they figure out the fastest way to get past an obstacle. Other times, they enjoy creating more difficult stunts to test themselves.

## Vaulting

There are a few movements that are typical to most parkour. The most important is vaulting. Vaulting is when a parkour athlete jumps or dives over an obstacle by using their feet and hands. They may either push off the obstacle or not touch it at all. These are difficult moves and not something a beginner should do. There are many types of vaults, such as a dash vault. A dash vault is when a runner jumps feetfirst, then uses their hands in the middle of the jump to push up off and over the obstacle. In a lazy vault, the runner approaches the obstacle at a diagonal. Then they make a scissor kick over it, using one hand for support. A star vault is a spectacular cartwheel over an obstacle. A sky vault is an even more challenging one-handed cartwheel!

A parkour athlete uses their hands for support when they swing their legs sideways to vault a low wall.

# Kinetic Energy

The parkour athlete's kinetic energy is important for vaulting. Kinetic energy is the parkour athlete's mass multiplied by their velocity. The run to the obstacle creates it. When the parkour athlete kicks up into the air, they have angular momentum. This means that while they are going forward, they are also rotating. The rotation makes it easier to tuck their legs to their body or to their side, which helps them clear the obstacle. As the parkour athlete jumps, they follow a path of **projectile motion** in which they have horizontal velocity and vertical velocity. Horizontal velocity carries them over the ground. Vertical velocity lifts them into the air. The parkour athlete follows an arc shape as they rise. They push against the obstacle at the highest point. In that moment, they have potential energy which can turn into kinetic energy as they move toward the ground again.

## GETTING PHYSICAL: USING THE BODY

The human body is designed to walk on two legs. Most of the biggest muscles in the body are in the legs, which have to support the most weight. In parkour, athletes use their legs a lot but they also use their arms in vaults. They use their arms when grabbing the tops of walls to flip themselves up. This requires not only strong arms, but also an understanding of how the body works. The arms can act as levers. They must carefully position their arms and take advantage of inertia and momentum. When they do so, athletes can lift their body weight with their arms through a small amount of effort.

Some parkour moves require great strength. Many rely more on an understanding of the body's weight distribution and movement.

# Leaping and Landing

In arm jumps, athletes jump toward a wall with their feet. At the same time, they catch the top of the wall with their hands to pull themselves up.

The most amazing part of parkour is the way athletes seem to defy gravity and "run" up walls. They learn to land safely from heights that would cause most people to break their bones. They learn this from training. They also learn this from physics.

## Jumping Up...

Parkour athletes run at a wall and jump. They place a foot on the wall to push themselves higher so they can grab the top of the wall. This is called a vertical world run. The world record is 13 feet 1 inch (4 m). When two walls are close together, some athletes can climb up in a series of zigzag jumps that carry them to the top. The secret is a combination of momentum and friction. Momentum is the force that keeps the runner moving forward. Friction is the force generated between the runner's foot that is in contact with the wall and the wall itself. The foot gains grip, then the runner applies as much downward force to the wall as possible to push themselves upward. The frictional force created is perpendicular to the wall.

## ...and Jumping Down

Parkour athletes can leap from great heights without hurting themselves. This is because they are in good physical shape and they practice for hours. This is also because of physics. As they hit the ground, they land on the balls of their feet, and use their ankles to spread the shock of the impact through their bodies. They try to keep their bodies relaxed, but also ready. They aim to bounce on impact like a rubber ball. If it is possible, the athletes go into a forward diagonal roll. They roll from one shoulder, down and across their back, to the opposite hip. The hip has more flesh to absorb the shock. Athletes go straight into the roll when they land. The roll is so they can use the ground reaction force to propel themselves forward.

## GETTING PHYSICAL: OVERCOMING GRAVITY

When parkour athletes seem to defy gravity, it is an illusion. A human being cannot defy gravity. No one can hang in the air for more than a second. For most people, the longest time is about 0.53 seconds. Parkour athletes change their forward momentum into upward momentum through the angle at which the fronts of their feet push up from the wall. They get friction against the wall, and their legs act as levers that push their bodies upward.

# Urban Slacklining

Urban slacklining, or urbanlining, is a street sport that takes practice, concentration, and agility. Slacklining is like tightrope walking, but while tightropes are thin and stretched tight, slacklines are made of wider, flat webbing, which is tied so it is slack. This means the line stretches, shakes, and bounces like a trampoline, while the slackliner does jumps and handstands. Slacklining is always performed close to the ground.

## Using Bounce

Slacklining dates back to the late 1970s, when students Adam Grosowsky and Jeff Ellington started experimenting with walking on loose chains and ropes. Inspired by circus performers, but wanting to take fewer risks, they anchored their lines near the ground. They soon discovered that walking on flat climbing webbing allowed them to do tricks, such as juggling and jump mounts.

## Skill Sets

Slackliners can take part in a number of different activities. Timelining involves trying to stay on a slackline for as long as possible without falling. This takes focus and amazingly strong leg, arm, and body muscles.

Slacklining is practiced in city parks and on beaches, usually on a 2-inch (5 cm) wide line.

Taking these skills a step further is slackline yoga, in which challenging poses must be held for minutes at a time.

Tricklining combines stunts with slacklining. Trickliners do 360-degree turns, chest bounces, drop knees, and jumps from line to line.

## Slower Tipping

The key to balancing on a slackline is to lower the body's center of mass toward the webbing. Leaning forward will affect the slackliner's balance. So, instead, they stand up straight and lower their hips by bending their knees.

As the slackliner steps, the line bounces and spins, knocking the walker off balance. To prevent falling, the slackliner must increase their moment of inertia. The best way for the slackliner to do this is to spread out their mass by extending their arms. Any wobbling now happens more slowly, giving the slackliner time to correct their motions before starting to fall.

## SCIENCE WINS!

### TWIN TOWER TIGHTROPE

In 1974, French tightrope walker Philippe Petit secretly made his way to the top of the Twin Towers of the World Trade Center. These were the tallest towers in New York City at the time. Philippe set up an illegal steel cable between the two towers. The cable was a quarter of a mile (402 m) above the ground. Carrying a long pole for balance, Petit walked back and forth between the towers eight times. He knelt, laid down on the rope, and waved to people watching below. The long pole helped stop him from tipping.

# CHAPTER 6

# BALL GAMES

**M**ost street games are only for fun. But, that does not mean that science is any less serious!

## Street Variations

There is a street version of almost every sport. Without a basketball court, people shoot at one hoop. Without soccer nets, they kick a ball against a wall. Walls also act as courts for handball. Handball is when players take turns hitting a ball against a wall with their hands. It is like racquetball without the racquets. For people who cannot get to an ice rink, roller hockey is also an option. It is like hockey but uses inline skates. Players hit a ball with their sticks instead of a flat puck.

Parks often have flat, smooth areas. With a pair of movable goal nets or a pair of jerseys for goalposts, they can be used for hockey.

There are so many versions of shooting hoops that you can play with almost any number of people. You can even play by yourself.

## Rolling Away

A ball rolls more easily than a puck. Friction slows the puck down, because the full face of the puck is dragging across the ground. A ball rolls more smoothly because only a small part of the sphere is in contact with the ground, so the friction on the ball reduces to almost nothing. A rubber ball has the chance to travel a long way on a smooth street. The hockey stick acts like a lever that multiplies the force of the player's hit. The force transfers to the ball. As Newton's First Law explains, unless there are other forces in the way, the ball can travel far. Part of the fun of playing ball games on the street is that there are often obstacles that are not faced in real sports, such as a bench in the middle of your stickball diamond. Players can use their balance to move around obstacles. They can also use their imagination to figure out ways to get the ball around them, such as flicking it over them.

# Stickball

**N**ot everyone gets to play baseball on a diamond. In many towns and cities, there is not enough space. The answer is stickball. This game is usually played with a piece of wood and a rubber ball or tennis ball. (The tennis ball is why the game is sometimes also called fuzzball.) Players pitch and swing. They try to run around bases that are usually urban features, such as fire hydrants or a particular stairway. There are no real rules and no set number of players. It is more fun for everyone if the sides are roughly equal and if all players take a turn to pitch and bat the ball.

A player keeps their eye on the ball for a catch during a stickball game in New York City.

## Baseball Physics

The physics of stickball are like the physics of baseball, but everything is a little slower, softer, or lighter. The bat acts as a lever as the batter swings, which creates torque, or rotational force. If the bat hits the ball, the forward velocity of the swing transfers to the ball. That uses the momentum of the bat to stop the momentum of the ball, then gives momentum in the opposite direction. There are two ways change an object's momentum like this. The first is applying a small force over a long time. The second is applying a large force for a short time. The bat and ball are in contact for only two milliseconds. So, the batter must generate a lot of force to make a home run.

The law of the conservation of momentum says that momentum before and after a collision must be the same. In this case, the combined momentum of the bat and ball before contact must equal their combined momentum after contact. The bat transfers much of its momentum to the ball, so it slows down while the ball speeds up and flies off.

## Key Differences

For the pitcher, it is harder to get a rubber ball or tennis ball to swing like a leather ball. The balls do not have the stitching. The stitching helps the pitcher use the friction of their grip to make a baseball spin in the air. There is another important difference between stickball and baseball. In the street, players do not slide into bases. That would only lead to torn pants!

## GETTING PHYSICAL: SCIENCE OF THE SWING

Often when you hit a ball with a stick, the ball goes straight up in the air or down along the ground. Their surfaces usually meet at different angles because they are different shapes. The ball is round and the stick is cylindrical. This causes the ball to fly at weird angles. That is why batters try to find the "sweet spot," where the precise center of the bat hits the precise center of the ball. In the 2 milliseconds they are together, the bat transfers maximum energy to the ball. They have to do this at the right angle to make sure the ball flies up and away.

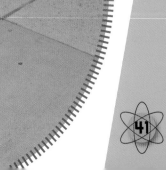

A young player warms up for their turn at bat by swinging a broom handle at a small rubber ball.

# Pickup Games

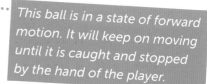

A lmost any sport can be played on the street or an urban court. There is usually less space, more or fewer players, and fewer rules than in the original game, but the basics remain the same. That means the science remains the same, too.

## Ideal for Ball Games

In street games, the surfaces tend to be quite hard and flat. These surfaces make them perfect for games in which balls have to roll and bounce. When a ball rolls along a flat surface, it follows the First Law of Motion. Once a ball is set in motion during a game of street hockey, it will remain in motion in the same direction. The motion will continue until an external force changes it. This quality is called inertia. It is what makes a still ball remain still and a rolling ball roll until it is slowed by the forces of gravity and friction.

This ball is in a state of forward motion. It will keep on moving until it is caught and stopped by the hand of the player.

# Make It Bounce

In games in which the ball bounces, the main physics ideas are potential energy and kinetic energy. When the ball is in a player's hand, it has potential energy, or the ability to do work, because of the force of gravity. If the ball drops, that potential energy turns to kinetic energy, or the energy of motion. If the ball bounces, it gets even more kinetic energy.

When a ball bounces off the floor (or on the wall in handball), it loses some of its kinetic energy in the bounce. The laws of physics say that energy cannot be destroyed or created, so the energy from the ball has to go somewhere else. In this case, the energy turns into heat energy, which is created by friction between the ball and the surface. That means the ball travels back from the bounce a little slower than it was going before the bounce. A player has to generate more force with their hands to keep it moving.

## GETTING PHYSICAL: ANGLES AND BOUNCE

Whenever a ball bounces, remember two physics ideas: incidence and reflection. Incidence is the angle at which the ball strikes the floor or wall. Reflection is the angle at which it bounces back off the floor or wall. The law of reflection says that the angle of incidence always equals the angle of reflection. If you bounce the ball a long way in front of you, it will bounce up again even farther ahead of you. If you bounce it straight down, it will bounce straight up to your hand again.

# GET PHYSICAL!

It is time to find out for yourself about the science of street sports. In this experiment, you will learn about momentum. The experiment needs at least two people, so find a friend or a group of friends to help.

## YOU WILL NEED:

- Skateboard
- Helmet and protective pads for elbows and knees
- 10-pound (4.5 kg) object, such as a heavy backpack
- Video camera or phone camera for recording

## Instructions

**1**. Have one person who is an experienced skateboarder put on the helmet and protective pads. Then have them stand on the skateboard in a flat, open space.

**2**. Make sure the camera is set up so it can record the person on the skateboard. Or, have a third person hold the camera.

**3**. Standing close to one end of the skateboard, gently toss the object to the person on the the skateboard.

Record a video of what happens when they catch it.

**4**. Repeat the experiment.

**5**. Now change the experiment around. Start with the person on the skateboard holding the object. Have them toss it gently to you. As they toss the object, film what happens to the skateboard.

**6**. Repeat the experiment.

**7**. Watch your results on video. It might help to watch on a large screen.

Make sure that the person on the skateboard has their weight spread out, with their feet over the axles.

## Analysis

Did the skateboard move when the person standing on it caught the object? What happened to the skateboard when the person on it tossed the object? Why do you think that might be?

## Conclusion

When a heavy object is thrown, it has momentum. Momentum is the amount of motion it has as a result of the combination of its mass and velocity.

Momentum is constant, unless external forces act upon it. When you toss the object to the person on the skateboard, it stops, but its momentum moves to the catcher. The momentum causes the skateboard to roll. When the person on the skateboard tosses the object, there will be an equal and opposite reaction. This is based on Newton's Third Law. Based on this law, if they throw the object forward, the thrower and the skateboard will be pushed backward.

# GLOSSARY

**accelerate** Change velocity by speeding up, slowing down, or changing direction while in motion

**aerodynamics** The study of how shapes reduce drag from the air

**air resistance** A force that acts in the opposite direction of an object traveling through the air, slowing it down

**angular momentum** The amount of rotation of an object

**axis** An imaginary line around which an object rotates

**axle** A rod that passes through the center of a wheel

**bearings** Small metal balls that support turning parts of a machine

**center of mass** The point in the middle of an object's mass

**centripetal force** A force that pulls a revolving object toward the axis of revolution

**cylindrical** A shape with a circular cross-section

**derbies** Sporting contests

**drag** A force that opposes an object's motion

**elasticity** Being able to stretch, then return to the original form

**flexible** Able to bend easily without breaking

**forces** Interactions that change the motion of something

**friction** The resistance of one object moving over another

**gravity** A force that attracts things toward the center of Earth, or toward any other physical body

**gyroscopic** Related to the energy of a spinning disk

**impact** The action of one object hitting another

**inertia** The quality of a moving body that makes it stay in motion or in a stationary body that makes it stay still

**kinetic energy** The energy an object has because of its motion

**levers** Bars resting on a pivot; used to move loads

**mass** The quantity of matter in an object, or its "weight"

**molecules** Particles formed by atoms bonding together

**moment of inertia** A measure of resistance to rotational movement

**momentum** The quantity of motion of a moving body, a product of its mass and velocity

**perpendicular** At a right angle to something

**physics** The branch of science that studies materials and energy

**pivots** To turn or spin on a central point

**polyurethane** An artificial type of resin

**potential energy** The energy possessed by an object because of its mass and position

**projectile motion** The motion of an object thrown near Earth's surface and moving in a curved path under the action of gravity

**rolling resistance** The force that stops a ball from rolling on a surface

**streamlined** Shaped to move smoothly through air or water

**terminal velocity** The fastest speed an object can reach under the force of gravity

**torque** The force that causes objects to rotate around an axis

**velocity** Speed in a specific direction

# LEARNING MORE

Find out more about the physics of street sports.

## Books

Becker, Helaine. *Skateboarding Science* (Sports Science). Crabtree Publishing, 2009.

Butler, Erin K. *Extreme Land Sports* (Sports to the Extreme). Capstone Press, 2017.

Jackson, Demi. *Roller Derby* (Daredevil Sports). Gareth Stevens Publishing, 2015.

Torres, John A. *Racing Soap Box Derby Stock Cars* (Speed Racers). Enslow Publishers Inc., 2018.

## Websites

Find out about the scientific ideas behind parkour at:
https://adventure.howstuffworks.com/outdoor-activities/
    urban-sports/parkour.htm

Discover how skateboarders perform their tricks at:
www.exploratorium.edu/skateboarding/trick.html

There are instructions for setting up a game of stickball at:
www.howcast.com/videos/how-to-play-stickball

Read an article about skating by a skater who is also a physicist at:
http://howeverythingworks.org/journal/Article1.2.pdf

# INDEX